MW00535141

SUCCEEDING WITH THE MASTERS®

ROMANTIC ERA, Volume One

Compiled and edited by Helen Marlais

About the Series

Succeeding with the Masters® is a series dedicated to the authentic keyboard works of the Baroque, Classical, Romantic, and Twentieth-Century masters.

This series provides a complete and easily accessible method for learning and performing the works of the masters. Each book presents the works in historical perspective for the student, and provides the means and the motivation to play these pieces in the correct stylistic, musical, and technical manner. The easily understandable format of practice strategies and musical concepts make this series enjoyable for both students and teachers.

To ensure authenticity, all of these pieces have been extensively researched. Teachers will find a wealth of excellent repertoire that can be used for recitals, festivals, competitions, and state achievement testing. Many of these original compositions may be new to you while others will be familiar. This series brings together an essential and comprehensive library of the pedagogical repertoire of the great composers.

Succeeding with the Masters® begins with late-elementary repertoire, continues through intermediate-level works and also includes a few early-advanced works. Upon completion of this series, students will be well prepared for the entry-level sonatas by the master composers.

THE
F·J·H
MUSIC
COMPANY
INC.

Production: Frank J. Hackinson
Production Coordinators: Philip Groeber and Isabel Otero Bowen
Cover: Terpstra Design, San Francisco – in collaboration with Helen Marlais
Text Design and Layout: Susan Pinkerton
Engraving: Tempo Music Press, Inc.
Printer: Tempo Music Press, Inc.

ISBN 1-56939-541-1

Copyright © 2005 The FJH Music Company Inc.
2525 Davie Road, Suite 360, Fort Lauderdale, Florida 33317-7424
International Copyright Secured. All Rights Reserved. Printed in U.S.A.
WARNING! The music, text, design, and graphics in this publication are protected by copyright law.
Any duplication is an infringement of U.S. copyright law.

PREFACE

A Note for Teachers and Students

Succeeding with the Masters®, Romantic Era Volume One, is a collection of graded repertoire featuring the great masters of the Romantic era. These works build a foundation for playing more advanced romantic music. Each piece is introduced by a short "discovery" of a particular characteristic of the Romantic era. "Practice strategies" guide the student in preparing and performing each piece. This comprehensive approach to learning style, technique, and historical context provides a valuable foundation for successful performance of all romantic repertoire pieces.

Characteristics of the Romantic Era

Two icons are used throughout the volume:

indicates the Musical Characteristics of the Romantic era.

Practice Strategy

outlines a practice strategy or illustrates a musical concept that guides the student in how to learn more efficiently and play more musically.

Many published collections take great liberties in altering pitches, rhythms, and articulations. The pieces in this collection, however, are based on Urtext editions, which are editions that reflect the composer's original intent. From these Urtext scores, the editor has created performance scores for the student. Markings that were not clearly intended by the composer are referenced at the bottom of the pieces.

- Fingerings have been added by the editor.
- Some articulations and interpretive dynamic markings have been added to guide students as they explore the romantic style.
- Editorial metronome markings are added as a guide.
- The CD includes complete performances and a practice strategy workshop. For a complete listing of track numbers, see page six.

MUSIC DURING THE ROMANTIC ERA (1800–1900)

Some of the romantic composers, such as Schubert, followed the footsteps of the classicists, using traditional forms and titles with more colorful and adventurous harmonies. Other composers forged ahead and were interested in writing works with programmatic titles, which meant that titles were supplied that produced a mental image. Imagery and feeling were very important during this era. Romantic composers were interested in nature, in the fantastical, and above all, in personal emotion. Emotional states such as love, sadness, joy and despair fueled creativity. The soloist became the dominant figure of the era, with pianists and violinists taking center stage. Whereas some composers were interested in writing intimate pieces for small instrumental groups and solo instrumentalists, others wrote large orchestral works for many instrumentalists.

Many revolutions took place in 1848, the year that Schumann's *Album for the Young* was composed. In Paris, Vienna, Budapest, Prague, Venice, and Milan, people fought for freedom and economic equality, with lasting effects on Europe. The middle class developed, and the members of this new social stratum became the main audience for classical music. In Vienna, for example, during the early part of the 1800s, citizens would go to operas and then would spend time with friends and family around a piano at home — playing, singing, and listening to music. Since there were no radios, televisions, or computers, the main entertainment was playing and listening to live music, which was featured in theme parks, city parks, coffee houses, and theatres. Balls (formal dances) were extremely popular. In 1832, 772 balls were held in Vienna alone and half of the population attended, dancing the ever-popular waltz!

MUSICAL CHARACTERISTICS OF THE ROMANTIC ERA:

- Emotion and drama are important aspects of the music.

- Some pieces are programmatic, meaning they tell a story or create an image in the mind that corresponds to the title of the piece.

- A strong sense of tonic to dominant movement in the harmony still exists. However, the harmonic language is expanded for added color through sound, using not only tonic, subdominant and dominant chords, but also chords that are not part of the key.

- Use of *rubato* introduces flexibility within the tempo, stretching or broadening and then pressing the tempo forward within the same phrase or shortly thereafter.

- Many pieces incorporate melodies with an accompaniment. However, the texture is often more dense and involved, with the melody and accompaniment often found in the same hand and a *countermelody* or accompaniment in the other hand. In the Classical era, one hand often had the melody and the other, the accompaniment.

- Pieces are sometimes meant to teach an aspect of technique or a musical concept.

- Phrases can be of varying lengths.

- Homophonic texture is featured, as well as the use of countermelodies.

- Ornamentation is used. Trills and turns are played *before* the beat, or between beats. (See the Baroque and Classical books of *Succeeding with the Masters®* to examine the difference.)

- New dynamic markings are created during this era for greater expression and drama, such as the *espressivo* marking. Romantic era music uses frequent *crescendos, decrescendos,* and sudden dynamic changes.

- Some composers use the traditional forms and symmetrical phrases known in the Classical era — (AB), (ABA), and Rondo, for example — but expand the harmonic language to use more colorful and adventurous harmonies.

- Some composers use traditional titles from the Baroque and Classical eras such as *Ecossaise, Sonata, German Dance, Minuet, Gavotte, Prelude, Theme and Variations.*

What the student will learn in Volume One:

Characteristics of the era:

S<small>CHUBERT</small> <small>PIECES</small>:
Schubert enjoyed using traditional forms and titles, so many of the characteristics of his writing are different from those of Schumann and Tchaikovsky.

S<small>CHUMANN</small> <small>PIECES</small>:
All of these pieces are programmatic, meaning they tell a story or create an image in the mind.

T<small>CHAIKOVSKY</small> <small>PIECES</small>:
All of these pieces are programmatic, meaning they tell a story or create an image in the mind.

Helen Marlais' Practice Strategies™:

Volume One – Late Elementary through Intermediate Repertoire

The pieces within each composer category are arranged in order of difficulty, with the least difficult pieces immediately following the short biography of the composer.

For a complete list of sources for these pieces, see page 86.

FRANZ SCHUBERT
(1797–1828)

Franz Schubert was born in Vienna, Austria, in 1797, just outside the city center. He began his life in a small apartment in a house that you can still see today. In a one-bedroom apartment, with one fireplace as its lone source of heat, lived Franz, his father, his mother, his brothers Ignaz, Ferdinand, and Karl, and his sister Maria Theresa! Schubert's father was from the small European country of Moravia. He was a school teacher, an occupation that had very little social standing, and limited financial reward. When Franz was four years old, the family moved to a house where the bottom floor was his father's school and the upper floor was their home. Franz started his schooling when he was six, and he was a high achiever. In those days, by imperial decree, all students learned their studies by rote, which means that they memorized everything by repetition, and were required to recite exactly what they had memorized.

After school, Franz's life was filled with music. His older brother Ignaz was his first piano teacher. His father taught him how to play the violin. His first teacher outside the family was Michael Holzer, who taught him to sing, and to play the organ. Holzer once commented that Franz already knew everything that he was trying to teach him! By the early age of thirteen, Franz had composed songs, string quartets, and piano pieces.

When it was obvious that Franz was very gifted, he auditioned to become the pupil of a famous composer and musician by the name of Antonio Salieri. Franz was engaged as a soprano in the boy's choir of the "Hofkapelle," the "Imperial High Chapel," which was supervised by Salieri. Franz received free tuition and board at the Imperial and Royal City College, a school taught by monks for boys from age eleven to an age when they were mature enough to enter the university. He spent five years studying at the school, where he played second violin in the school orchestra, and where he was introduced to the works of Haydn, Mozart, and Beethoven.

Schubert was known for his beautiful, rich melodies and his interesting harmonic language. He also liked to use traditional forms and titles. You can hear and see these characteristics of Schubert's style in the piano pieces in this volume.

A man named Otto Deutsch researched and organized all of Schubert's works. The abbreviation D associated with a title stands for his last name. The D numbers list all of Schubert's works in chronological order.

Ecossaise in C major

An *écossaise* is a country dance played in a quick $\frac{2}{4}$ meter.
This piece is from a set of eight *écossaises*, composed in Austria
on October 3, 1815. Elsewhere in the world, the first commercial
cheese factory was opened in Switzerland.

Characteristics of the Romantic Era

Some romantic composers, Schubert among them, enjoyed using traditional forms. Many of Schubert's écossaises have a binary form (AB). Mark AB in your score (with a pencil!).

Practice Strategy

The importance of "hands-alone" work:

As you begin learning this piece, practice it hands apart. If any of the reaches are too large for your hands, omit the notes that are in parentheses. You can choose your fingering once you and your teacher decide what to do about these particular notes.

Measures 7-8, left hand:
Do these two measures feel better with or without the lower G on the second beat?

Measure 16, right hand:
Is this measure easier to play with or without the lower C on the first beat?

Let the phrase marks be a guide for you when you practice hands separately. By concentrating on the phrasing, the fingering will make a great deal of sense, because within each slur you will see a pattern.

Similar pattern, starting 1 step higher.

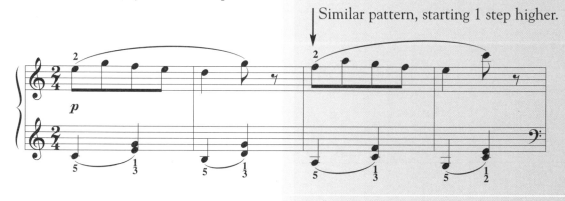

Ecossaise in C major

Franz Schubert
D. 299, No. 8

(a) The low G may be omitted if played by a smaller hand.

N.B. The long slurs in measures 5–8, 9–10, and 13–14 show the longer phrases and are editorial.

FF1440

GERMAN DANCE IN A MAJOR

No one knows exactly when Schubert composed this lovely dance,
but it was published in 1889, more than sixty years after his death.
Many world events occurred when it was published. The George
Washington Bridge opened in the United States, linking New Jersey
with New York; In Paris, the Eiffel Tower was completed.

Characteristics of the Romantic Era

Romantic composers often used more chromaticism in their pieces than classical composers did. "Chromaticism" refers to the use of notes that are half steps apart. Play the following A major scale, and then a chromatic scale starting on A, circling the pitches that are *not* part of the A major scale.

A major scale:

Chromatic scale beginning on A:

Play measures three to eight of the German Dance, shown below. The chromatic notes are circled. Chromatic tones lend an interesting sound change, or add *color* to a piece of music.

Practice Strategy

"Play-prepare":

In order to play the left-hand accompaniment well, be sure to lift from the keyboard immediately after playing the downbeat, and *prepare* the second beat. Look ahead for what notes come next, so that you are able to place the correct fingering over the correct keys, like this:

Measures 1-4:

Lift your left hand and prepare the second beat.

When you know for sure that the correct fingers are over the correct keys, then you can play the notes.

Now try the same strategy, this time hands together. With practice, you will be able to "feel" where the leaps are in the left hand, and you'll be free to watch where your right hand is going.

GERMAN DANCE IN A MAJOR

Franz Schubert
D. 972, No. 3

N.B. The slurs are Schubert's own, except for m. 12.

* An easier way to play is the following:

ECOSSAISE IN G MAJOR

This piece was composed in 1821. Just one year later, in 1822, the Royal Academy of Music was founded in London. What interesting musical feature in this *écossaise* makes it sound like a country dance? Listen to the CD recording to help you identify it.

Characteristics of the Romantic Era

In this piece, Schubert uses mostly tonic (I), subdominant (IV), and dominant (V) harmonies. Mark these harmonies in your full score.

tonic (I)   subdominant (IV6/4)   dominant seventh (V7)

Practice Strategy

Practicing scale patterns:
Mark the two places in your full score where you see a D major scale pattern (measures five and thirteen). In order to play these with ease, try the following:

Practice the following D major scale by repeating it four times in a row correctly.

Now, take out the C♯ at the top and add a C natural instead. Again, play this scale correctly four times.

Finally, add the leading tone (C♯) to the beginning of the scale.

Do you really know this scale? If so, you will be able to play it backwards, like this:

Practicing scale patterns backwards as well as forwards is a good test to see if your fingers really know the pattern. When your fingers know the patterns well, you will be able to play musically and with confidence!

ECOSSAISE IN G MAJOR

Franz Schubert
D. 145, No. 4

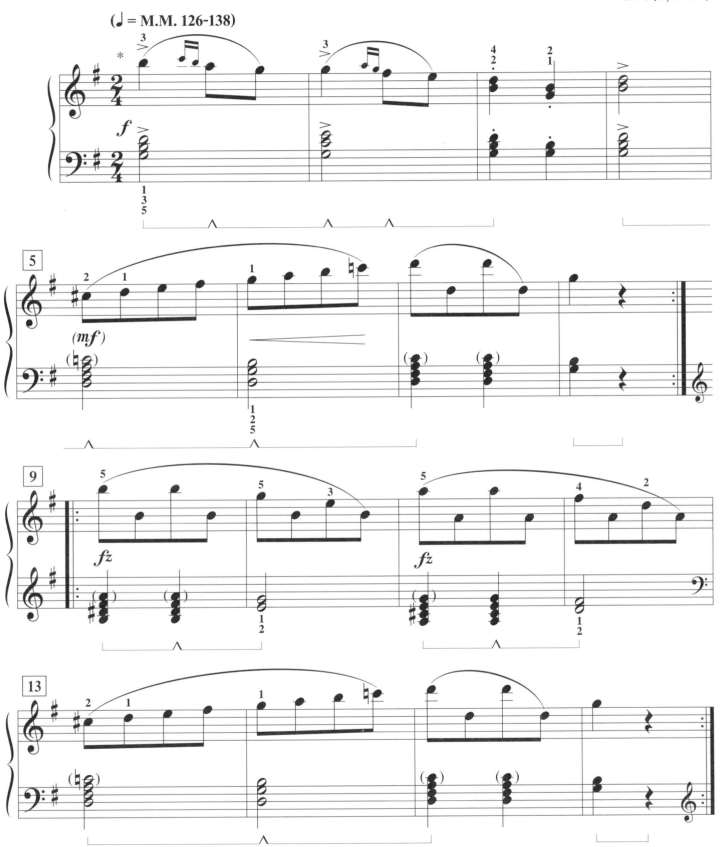

*The smaller notes in measures one and two are played on the "and" after the first beat.

N.B. The notes in parentheses may be omitted if played by a smaller hand and the chord can be played with fingers 5, 3, 1.

LÄNDLER IN G MAJOR

This piece is from a collection titled, 36 Original Dances/First Waltzes.
A Ländler is usually in ¾ time, and it is a slow dance from Austria.

Characteristics of the Romantic Era

For some romantic composers, the influence of the Classical era is evident in their compositions that have symmetrical, four-bar phrases. Look at the score on the next page and mark the symmetrical phrases with large parentheses. The first phrase is shown below.

Notice that the last phrase of the piece is eight measures long instead of four, and that it makes up the entire B section. When you play this longer phrase, feel its energy and forward momentum. This longer phrase and the emotion it conveys as it builds intensity show that the piece is indeed romantic, even though the form is classical. Listen to the practice strategy on the CD recording in order to fully understand this characteristic.

Practicing two-note slurs:

Practice Strategy

The prevalence of two-note slurs in this dance creates an image in our mind of what it was like to listen to folk music in the Austrian countryside during the1800s. Playing these slurs is essential in bringing this piece to life.

This is how to achieve an excellent sound in the two-note slurs:

1) Let your wrist drop and relax on the first note of the two-note slur. (See the illustration below.) This motion helps your wrist be more flexible, and you will create a better sound. Try not to overdo the drop or you will feel unnecessary tension. Your teacher can help you with this at your lesson.

2) On the second note of the slur, raise your wrist until it is level with your arm. The second note of the slur should sound lighter than the first note.

3) As you play this last note of the slur, continue to lift your wrist while rolling up on your thumb until you are playing the key with the fleshy part of your finger. Remember to roll your finger and wrist towards the fallboard of the piano.

Drop your wrist here   Lift and roll your wrist here

This technical motion is essential for playing two-note slurs. Practice this until it feels secure and comfortable. The key to success is to always listen to the sound that you produce. The second note should always sound lighter than the first.

LÄNDLER IN G MAJOR

Franz Schubert
D. 365, No. 21

(a) The trill should be played *before* the beat.

LÄNDLER IN B FLAT MAJOR

This Ländler is from the set *Eight Ländler,* composed in February of 1816. Schubert was known for writing beautiful melodies, and we can clearly hear a lovely melody in this dance. Also in the year 1816, Sir David Brewster invented the kaleidoscope in England, while in the United States, Indiana became the nineteenth state.

Characteristics of the Romantic Era

Beautiful melodies with a simple accompaniment were common in the Romantic era as they were in the Classical era. During the Romantic era, composers used more colorful harmonies in the accompaniment. This texture is called *homophonic.* Homophonic texture can also refer to a piece in which all of the parts move in rhythm and in a chordal style. Compare the differences illustrated below:

Monophonic texture
(one melodic line)

Homophonic texture
(melody and accompaniment)

Polyphonic texture
(two important lines)

Practice Strategy

Using half and quarter pedal:

You might find that in the A section, where the pedal is not marked, you can apply some half or quarter pedal. You can experiment with pressing the pedal only halfway down, and then only a quarter of the way down on every downbeat in this section. This kind of pedaling helps to add resonance to the sound while keeping the notes of the melodic line clear.

Practice Strategy

Playing a measure written for a large hand:

In order to make the left-hand accompaniment easier in the B section of this piece, try the following: Instead of holding onto the first note of every measure for three beats, hold it only for one beat and use the pedal to sustain the bass.

B section:

Now this section will be easy for you and you will be able to play the Ländler with exuberance!

Ländler in B flat major

Franz Schubert
D. 378, No. 3

con pedale

*The slurs from measures nine to sixteen are editorial, as well as the upbeat to m.1; and m.2, 4, and 6 third beats.
(a) The low F may be omitted if played by a smaller hand.
(b) The top F may be omitted if played by a smaller hand.

WALTZ IN B MINOR

The name "waltz" originates from the German word, "walzer," which means "to turn." In dance, the waltz has an accented first beat, and then a turn that follows. Peasants in Austria created the waltz, but soon people of all social tiers enjoyed it and made it fashionable.

Characteristics of the Romantic Era

Schubert was a master at using major and minor tonalities within the same piece. Listen to the CD recording and notice how he juxtaposes B minor tonality with B major tonality in measures 24 to 25. This change in tonality is a magical musical surprise to the ear.

Measures 23-28:

Practice Strategy

Perfect rhythm:

If the dotted rhythms in this waltz are played accurately, it will sound elegant and energetic. If the rhythm is not accurate, the waltz will sound lazy and tired. Look at the dotted rhythms in the beginning of the piece.

Measures 1-4:

Count and clap the following sixteenth-note patterns:

Now count and clap a triplet rhythm instead:

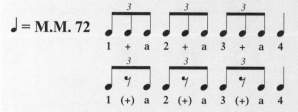

When you practice this piece, be sure to use this rhythm ♪♬ and not, ♪♬³.

**Practice
Strategy**

Creating the mood of the piece:

This piece has an intimate feel, especially since Schubert marked the beginning *pianissimo*. Even though there are accents on many of the beats, feel these as slight dramatic inflections, not as percussive accents. Listen to the CD to hear this interesting feature of this piece.

The only other place in this waltz where Schubert marks a *pianissimo* is at the recapitulation in measure 25, shown below.

Since this is the first time your audience will hear major tonality instead of minor tonality, you can linger a bit longer in measure 24 to prepare the listener for the surprise tonality in measure 25. It will be a real eye-and ear-opener!

Viennese Waltz

Waltz in B minor

Franz Schubert
D. 145, No. 6

N.B. The dynamics in measures 3, 4, 11, and 12 are editorial.

LÄNDLER IN G MAJOR

**This Ländler is from a set entitled *Homage aux belles Viennoises,*
which means, "homage to the beautiful Viennese women."**

**Characteristics
of the
Romantic Era**

Schubert enjoyed using traditional forms, perhaps because he played so much of the music of Haydn, Mozart, and Beethoven when he was in school. In this piece, we see a simple ternary form (ABA). In ternary form, there is a middle section (B) that has different melodic material than the outer A sections. Mark this form directly in your score. Write three ways the B section is different from the A section.

1) _____

2) _____

3) _____

**Practice
Strategy**

"8 times to perfection":

In this practice strategy, the focus is on playing the same section perfectly many times in a row. With the metronome set to a comfortable tempo, play a segment that you and your teacher have identified. Once you have played the segment, count two beats before you begin the segment again, as illustrated below.

In order to learn pieces well, make sure that you concentrate on playing the segment with one hundred percent accuracy and that you play the segment eight times *correctly*. Remember, practicing *begins* when you play the segment *correctly*. Say the number of each repetition out loud each time you begin the section again and focus on making musical phrases. Listen to the practice strategy on the CD to further understand this concept.

Continue to practice sections of this piece (you can create your own starting and stopping places!) using this practice strategy. Practice slowly, then *a tempo*, and you will be able to play this Ländler flawlessly.

Schubert and his friends

LÄNDLER IN G MAJOR

Franz Schubert
D. 734, No. 4

(a) The top D may be omitted if played by a smaller hand.

ped. simile

WALTZ IN A MAJOR

By the time Schubert was a teenager in his native Vienna, the waltz was extremely popular and people danced it all of the time. Waltzes are always in triple meter with the feeling of one large beat divided into three little beats. They have a joyful character, whether they are slow or fast.

Characteristics of the Romantic Era

Different dynamics are often heard within the same piece, creating drama.

Measures 1 to 8 are one long phrase:

Measures 9 to 16 are the second phrase.

Listen to the CD recording and add the following dynamics in your full score:

1) Add crescendo signs when you hear the dynamic level increase.

2) Find the phrase goals in these two phrases (m. 1-8 and 9-16) and mark them. (Remember the phrase goal is the place towards which the music naturally moves; after the goal, the music tapers in dynamic.)

3) You will hear the second eight-measure phrase begin *mezzo forte* and get louder to the end of the waltz. These dynamics are editorial. You can experiment with adding your own dynamic markings in the second phrase and see which you prefer to play.

Bringing a piece to life musically after it is learned:

Listen to the CD recording of this piece, and describe what kind of a feeling this waltz displays.

Practice Strategy

Circle the three adjectives below that best describe this piece:

haughty   *happy*   *lucky*

lonely   *harsh*   *spirited*

Can you add one more adjective to explain the emotion of this piece?_____

Think about these adjectives every time you sit down to practice or perform this piece!

Waltz in A major

Franz Schubert
D. 365, No. 16

(a) The turn at the beginning of the piece and in measure 4 should be played before the beat.
N.B. The dynamics in measures 9–16 are editorial, as well as the slurs.

ROBERT SCHUMANN

(1810-1856)

Robert Schumann was born in Germany, in the small city of Zwickau, near Dresden. He began to study piano when he was young, and started to compose when he was only eleven years old. Schumann's father was a writer and publisher. Because his parents wanted him to become a lawyer, at the age of eighteen he went to Leipzig University. He studied piano there with a teacher by the name of Friedrich Wieck, whose nine-year-old daughter Clara was destined to become one of the best musicians of the age.

When Robert was twenty, he decided to forgo his law studies and pour himself into music. Friedrich Wieck told Schumann that he could be a virtuoso performer. Unfortunately, Schumann injured his hand with a device he created to increase his reach. In 1834, probably inspired by his father's career, Schumann co-founded a newspaper, the *New Journal for Music*, which became one of the most influential music journals of the time.

Robert and Clara fell in love and were married in 1840, against her father's wishes. The master composers Frédéric Chopin, Felix Mendelssohn, and Johannes Brahms were their friends. Clara was a marvelous concert pianist and composer, and she influenced many composers of her day, who came to her for musical and compositional advice.

Schumann's first works were written for the piano. The pieces in this volume are all from his *Album for the Young*, which he composed in 1848. Six pieces from the collection were composed for his oldest daughter, Marie, and given to her as a present on her seventh birthday: "Soldiers' March," "Humming Song," "A Hymn," "Little Piece," "Poor Orphan Child," and "Little Hunting Song." Schumann continued to compose pieces that depicted the family life he and Clara shared with their seven children, until he had an album of forty-three pieces. Clara was very fond of Robert's compositions. She taught the easier pieces to their children, and we can assume that she played the more difficult works herself for the family to enjoy.

SOLDIERS' MARCH

This piece and all of the pieces by Schumann in this volume are from a collection entitled *Album for the Young*. The same year this collection was composed, revolutions occurred throughout Europe.

Some pieces are programmatic, which means that they tell a story, or create an image in the mind of the listener that relates to the title. This piece definitely sounds like the title, because the dotted rhythms create the feel of a march.

Characteristics of the Romantic Era

How to create a march:

A march has simple and strong rhythm, and regular phrasing. In order to feel this piece as a march, one must be sure that it is rhythmically accurate.

Practice Strategy

1) Tap and speak the subdivisions of the first measure, no faster than ♩ = MM. 66.

Right hand:

Left hand:

one (e and) a - two

2) Play the first measure without the slur and speak the subdivisions:

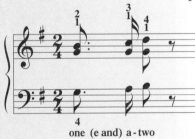

one (e and) a - two

3) Practice all of the measures with dotted rhythms in the same way.

4) Then play complete four-measure phrases with the slurs as written. Continue to speak the subdivisions and play with the metronome.

5) Remember that silences/rests are just as important as the notes you play. Speaking the subdivisions will help to keep the rests the correct length.

6) Next, play without speaking the subdivisions, but keep the metronome on. Ask yourself, "Does my rhythm sound like a march, with perfectly dotted rhythms and a steady beat?"

Soldiers' March

Robert Schumann
Op. 68, No. 2

Cheerfully and in strict tempo ($\quarternote$ = M.M. 96-104)

N.B. All eighth notes should be played *staccato*. The slurs are editorial as well as $\mathrel{<}$ and $\mathrel{>}$.

31

N.B. The dynamic markings in measures 19 and 21 are editorial.

THE WILD RIDER

The same year this piece was composed, the first telegraph link between
New York City and Chicago was formed.

**Characteristics
of the
Romantic Era**

Drama is an important aspect of music during the Romantic era. When Schumann wrote
this piece, he was thinking of a child riding on a toy stick horse. Robert's wife Clara
commented that the *sforzandos* (*sf*) in the music depict when the child is running into
the furniture and other objects!

**Practice
Strategy**

Playing two-note slurs:

In the initial stages of learning this piece, practice the hands separately, concentrating
on the melodic lines only. Drop forcefully into the first note of each two-note slur to
create the *sforzando* feel, and then immediately lift your wrist and come off the second
note of the slur. The second note of the slur should be *staccato* in order to prepare for the
staccato note after the two-note slur.

Schumann made a point of writing the *sf* (*sforzandos*) into the score. Use these *sforzandos*
as a smart guide — whenever you see one, remember to use the two-note slur technique
described in the paragraph above.

(♩. = M.M. 92-108)

Always listen to yourself when you practice, in order to hear the differences between the
staccato notes and the two-note slurs. The entire piece should be light and very clear.
The change in articulation combined with the *sforzandos* and brisk tempo help to create
the image of a young boy riding his toy horse.

**Practice
Strategy**

Practicing with the metronome:

Set the metronome at ♪ = M.M. 76. Practice the hands separately at first, then together.
Work on very small segments, such as one measure plus the next downbeat, or even only
half a measure (beats 1-4).

One measure plus one downbeat:

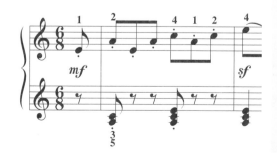

Half a measure:

Increase your speed gradually to ♩. = M.M. 76.

It is a good idea to stop on various beats to make sure you are lining up your playing with the tick of the metronome. Listen to the practice strategy on the CD recording to understand this fully.

When you are comfortable with this speed and know that you can play all of the notes accurately and rhythmically, you can increase the tempo, counting internally and feeling two beats to the bar at ♩. = M.M. 92-108. The metronome helps to develop your sense of inner pulse!

Boy at the piano

THE WILD RIDER

Robert Schumann
Op. 68, No. 8

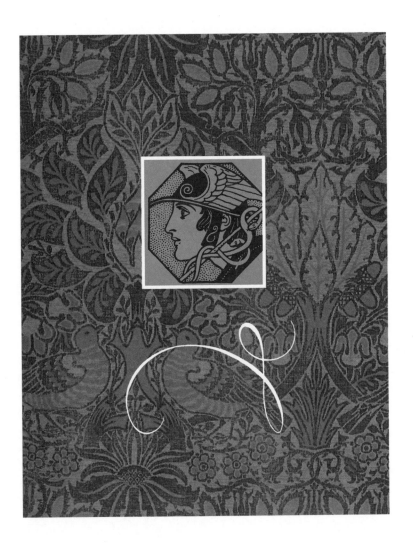

MELODY

In 1848, when this piece was composed, Franz Joseph I became Emperor of Austria and King of Hungary. That part of the world was called the Austro-Hungarian Empire.

Characteristics of the Romantic Era

Espressivo dynamic markings are an important way of emphasizing emotion in the music.

Measures 5-8:

Practice Strategy

Listen to the CD recording of this piece. What do you notice about the notes that have the *espressivo* marking <> over them? Circle below any of the sentences that describe the overall sound of these notes:

→ These notes are played more quietly than the other notes in the phrase.

→ More time is taken when playing these notes.

→ These notes are warmer and fuller than the notes around them.

→ These notes are in the same tempo as the rest of the phrase.

→ The tempo rushes when this note is reached.

Schumann used this *espressivo* dynamic marking to denote great expression. When you see this marking, press into the key, making it more special than the other notes within the same phrase. Play it with tenderness, emotion, and extra warmth. It not only indicates a change in dynamic, but also a stretching of the tempo at this point.

Keen listening:

The simplicity of this piece makes it intimate and beautiful. To create a magical sound, listen while you play, to be sure that your left hand and your right-hand notes are played exactly at the same time. If one hand comes in early or late, even for a split second, the magical sound will not be created because the clarity of the texture is muddied. Listen to the practice strategy on the CD recording to hear examples of how the piece should sound, and examples of how it should not sound!

Practice Strategy

It is very important that the rhythm in the two hands line up perfectly. If they do, you will create an enchanting sound as the melody and accompaniment float along perfectly together.

Boy sleeping under a tree

MELODY

Robert Schumann
Op. 68, No. 1

Three Musicians

FF1440

A Hymn

In many homes, people played familiar hymns from church.
This hymn was important to the Schumanns.

Practice Strategy

Practicing chordal pieces:

Imagine that a four-part vocal ensemble is singing this chorale. The soprano is the top voice, the alto sings the melodic line right below the soprano, and the tenor and the bass parts are found in the bass clef, as shown below:

Without using the pedal, enjoy practicing various voices together, but not all of the voices at once, like this:

1) Practice each voice by itself.
2) Practice tenor and bass together.
3) Practice alto and soprano together.
4) Then practice bass, tenor, and alto together.
5) Then practice bass, tenor, and soprano together.

Every time you practice, be sure to use the same fingering. This way, you will feel confident and will be able to play all four voices at the same time. Perhaps you can check off the numbers in the list above every time you practice this way. When you can play the voices *legato*, you can begin to add the pedal for a warm and sustaining sound. Remember that in cut time (¢), each ♩ gets one beat.

Even when you know this piece well, you can review the piece by taking the voices apart as described.

Adding your own dynamics:

Schumann only wrote one dynamic marking for the entire piece — a *piano* at the beginning. Decide where each phrase leads (the phrase goal), after which you can taper the sound for the end of the phrase. Notice that the second phrase feels as though it could build in volume. Decide how you would like the third and fourth phrases to sound — the same or different from the first two phrases?

A Hymn

Robert Schumann
Op. 68, No. 4

N.B. Alternate fingering for a smaller hand in measures 7 and 8:

HUMMING SONG

This piece was inspired by the youngest of the seven Schumann children.
Perhaps this piece was played when it was time for the infant to sleep.

**Characteristics
of the
Romantic Era**

Observe in this piece:

Use of a melody and a *countermelody*.

The first eight measures of this piece have a melody in the right hand and an accompaniment in the left hand.

Measures 1-6:

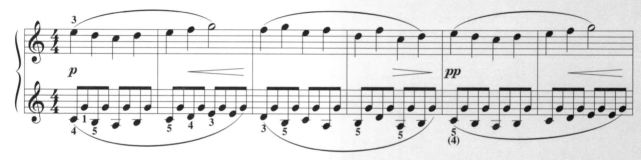

But in the B section, there is a melody and accompaniment within the same hand, and the left hand provides a secondary melody. This secondary melody is called a *countermelody*.

**Practice
Strategy**

Here are two ways to practice pieces that have a melody with an accompaniment and a countermelody.

1) Block only the right-hand like this:

Then add the left hand, continuing to block every beat:

2) Play the main melody and the countermelody without the accompaniment:

When you can play the two melodies together easily, then add the **inner accompaniment,** playing slowly:

Applying *rubato*:

Listen to the CD recording. Mark directly in your score where you hear flexibility in the tempo – first a broadening, or stretching of the tempo, and then, shortly thereafter, a return back to the previous tempo.

A good marking to use for the stretching of the tempo is this: ‿‿‿‿

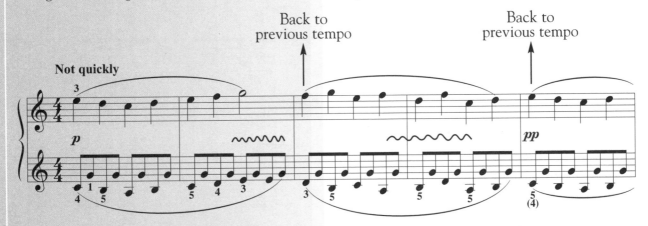

Rubato means to be flexible with the tempo, stretching or broadening and then pressing the tempo forward within the same phrase or shortly thereafter. The use of rubato during the Romantic era was customary, and this expressive way to play is something that you can start to learn now. Here's how:

1) Sing or hum the melody *while* you play and you will start to realize where you can take time.

2) Sing or hum the melody *away* from the piano, and the flexible rhythm will become part of you.

3) Practice the piece with a steady tempo, without taking any rubato. Play it with the metronome, around 80 to the quarter note. Then, turn off the metronome and add a beautiful rubato.

4) You can create words to sing along with the melody. Your teacher can help you with this to make the lyrics completely your own.

It is important to be able to play the piece in time, with the metronome, so that you can control your rubato. The rubato only works if you have established a clear and steady tempo to stretch or push against.

HUMMING SONG

Robert Schumann
Op. 68, No. 3

N.B. The tempo changes in measures 12, 13, and 24 are editorial.

N.B. All dynamic markings except for the ones in measures 1, 9, 16, and 17 are editorial.

FIRST LOSS

This piece was composed after a pet bird died in the Schumann household. Robert might also have been thinking about his first-born son who had passed away just a year before he composed his *Album for the Young*.

Characteristics of the Romantic Era

Characteristics of the Romantic era exemplified in this piece:

- ■ Emotion plays an important role.
- ■ More dynamic markings suggest even greater expression.

The expression of personal emotion is a very important characteristic of this era. Listen to the CD recording and answer the following question: Do you think this is a good title for this piece? If so, why? Let's imagine that Schumann is telling a story of loss through music.

Many of the phrases have dynamics marked in. Other phrases do not. Listening to the CD, add in all of the dynamics that you hear. Add *crescendo* and *decrescendo* signs, and mark in *piano*, *mezzo piano*, *mezzo forte*, and *forte* whenever you hear a change. Then, listen again to the piece and listen to the *fp* notes in the A section. This *forte-piano* marking adds to the overall expression of the piece.

Practice Strategy

Shaping phrases:

Each phrase in this piece is eight measures long. Mark these phrases in your full score, following what has been done for you in the A section below:

phrase 1

The phrasing is very interesting in the B section because where one long phrase ends, the next phrase starts, as shown below in measure 24:

Listening or playing the last four measures of the piece—what do you think is the emotion? (Choose two.)

depressed　　*serene*　　　　*calm*　　　　*excited*

scared　　　*sad*　　　　　*nervous*　　*mad*

Practice Strategy

Using half and quarter pedal:

When the pedal is marked, experiment with pressing the pedal only halfway down, and then only a quarter of the way down. You will notice that each different pedal technique lends a different sound, or color, to the music. You might find, through keen listening, that even where the pedal is not marked, you can apply some half or quarter pedaling.

First Loss

Robert Schumann
Op. 68, No. 16

*Measures 24 and 25 can be easily played as follows:

THE MERRY FARMER

When Schumann's collection *Album for the Young* was composed,
the first gaslights were installed in the White House of the United States.

**Characteristics
of the
Romantic Era**

Can you find the melody throughout this piece?

Listen to the CD recording and look at the full score.

1. Which hand has the melody at the beginning of the piece? _____

2. Starting with the upbeat to measure nine, both hands have a melody, as illustrated
   below. Draw a line from one melodic note to another, so that you can clearly see
   where the melody is, as compared to the accompaniment.

3. Where in the piece does the left hand again have the main melody only? _____

Energize the melody:

In order to convey the cheerful mood of this piece, it is important to "energize" your
fingers and make every note of the melody sing, as if your fingers are excited and doing
something they love!

When you see a phrase with a slur over it, think about where this phrase *leads*. The first
phrase actually leads to the second phrase that leads to the third phrase, making one long
phrase. So, without rushing, "energize" your fingers and listen to where the phrases go.

Upbeat to measure 1 through measure 4:

1 long phrase

**Practice
Strategy**

Using imagery to create a successful performance:

Sometimes it is helpful to create a story in your mind before you play the piece in front of an audience. In this way, you will be thinking of another fresh, new way to look at this piece. The full title of this piece is, *Merry Farmer, Returning from Work*.

Schumann's wife Clara came up with a story you can imagine about this piece:

In the beginning of the piece the farmer is singing merrily as he walks home from work. When both melodies appear, one of his young sons sings with him. Where in the music does the farmer sing alone again? _____

Can you create another image or story in your mind about this piece?

In the space provided below, pretend that you are the merry farmer and write your own story about the day.

THE MERRY FARMER

Robert Schumann
Op. 68, No. 10

N.B. The dynamic markings in the following measures are editorial: 2, 4, 6, 8, 10, and 14.

LITTLE STUDY

Characteristics of the Romantic Era

Practice Strategy

During the Romantic era, many small pieces were composed as technical studies in order to facilitate playing other, larger romantic works. A study usually focuses on only one or two technical or musical points. In this study by Schumann, the main lessons are to play very lightly and evenly throughout, with a *legato* touch, while bringing out the melody.

"Blocking" practice strategy:

In the initial stages of learning this piece, you may use this practice strategy to assist you in learning the fingering and the notes with great accuracy and precision. Start your practice by grouping the melody notes into chords. This helps you to see and feel the patterns of a piece more quickly than if you tried to learn the piece note by note.

Measures one to three, blocked:

Practice the blocked patterns until you feel secure with them. Then try blocking the rest of the piece!

Practicing to perform with the utmost evenness:

Practice Strategy

Using the metronome at ♩.=108, count out loud while you play. Stop on every fourth beat, as shown here:

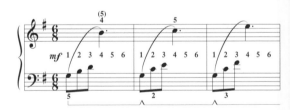

Then practice stopping on every first beat in a measure:

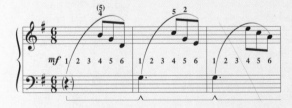

Always listen to make sure that the notes that are supposed to line up with the click of the metronome, clearly do. It might take repeated practice to get this "in your system," but it will be well worth the effort because once you do, you will be able to turn off the metronome and play this study skillfully, with complete evenness.

Now, count *two* beats per bar to keep the phrases moving in a forward direction. Listen to the practice strategy on the CD recording to fully understand this concept.

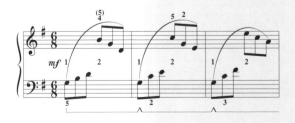

Little Study

Robert Schumann
Op. 68, No. 14

Lightly and very equally (♩. = M.M. 112-126)

*The pedaling is Schumann's, however, the pedal signs (└──^──┘) are the editor's.

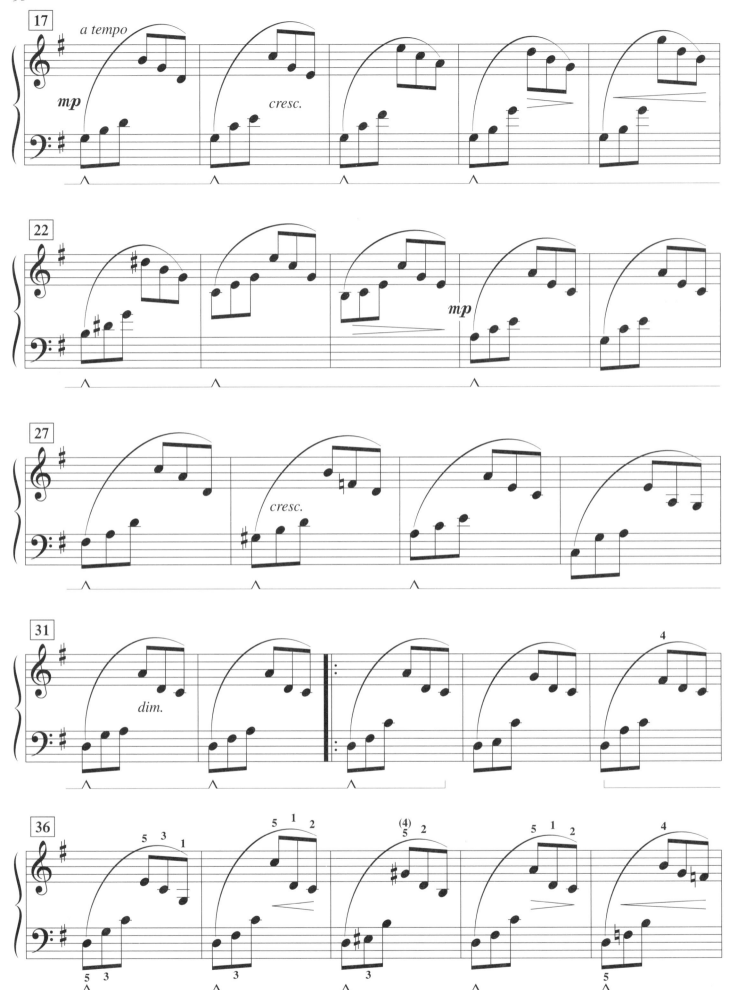

N.B. Schumann's own dynamic markings are in measures 5, 8, 21, 24, 31, 40, 42, 44 and 53.

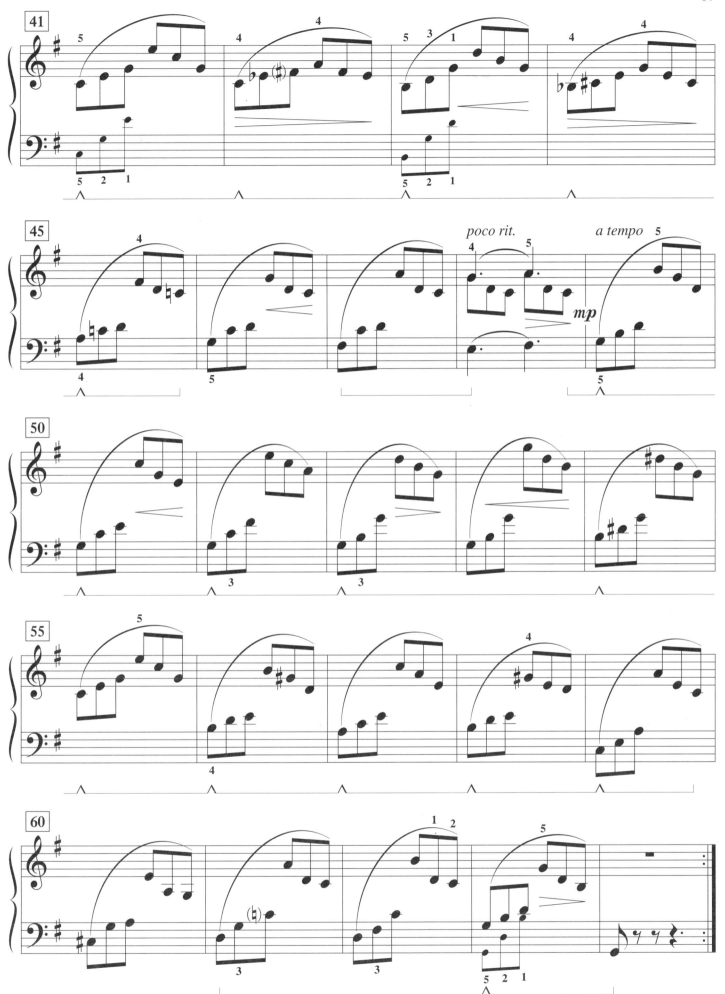

N.B. The smaller notes in measures 41, 43, and 63 are Schumann's alternates.
   The pedaling in measure 48 is editorial.

PETER TCHAIKOVSKY

(1840-1893)

Pyotr (Peter) Ilyich Tchaikovsky was born on May 7, 1840. He was the son of a mining inspector in the Urals, a mountain range that extends 1525 miles (2500 km) from north to south in Western Russia. Peter was the second of six children.

Growing up in Russia, Peter received a very good education from a French governess, as well as a local music teacher. At the age of ten, Peter's family moved to St. Petersburg, an important Russian city. His mother took him to see his first opera, an experience that changed Peter's life. Even though none of his family members had ever been professional musicians, Peter was drawn to the art. He was known as an extremely sensitive child, so music was a perfect outlet for his emotions. However, he graduated from a law school at the age of nineteen and became a government clerk, with music as only a secondary interest.

At the age of twenty-one, Peter decided that law was not for him. He wanted to immerse himself in music instead. He was accepted into a new music school established by Anton Rubinstein, who was one of the most famous pianists of the time. This school came to be known as the St. Petersburg Conservatory. Peter studied harmony, counterpoint, and composition, and in 1865 he not only graduated, but also won a silver medal for one of his choral pieces.

In 1866, Peter became Professor of Harmony at the Moscow Conservatory, and he busied himself with composition. He traveled extensively, making twenty-six trips to Paris, Berlin, Vienna, and New York City. In February of 1878, Tchaikovsky began to think about composing a set of pieces for young students. After he received permission from his publisher, he began to compose a *Children's Album* and in three days had finished the first sketches of all the pieces! Tchaikovsky's inspiration for the work was Robert Schumann's collection *Album for the Young,* which had been composed thirty years earlier.

In 1891, Tchaikovsky came to the United States and spent time in New York, Baltimore, and Philadelphia, leading four concerts of his works. These personal appearances may be why his music is so popular in the United States to this day. Tchaikovsky became the most popular composer in Russian during the Soviet regime, and officials urged other composers to follow in Tchaikovsky's footsteps. His most famous pieces are those that you are probably already familiar with: *The Nutcracker Suite, Swan Lake, Romeo and Juliet,* and *Sleeping Beauty.* The pieces in this collection are from his *Children's Album.*

Photo: akg-images.London

THE SICK DOLL

Tchaikovsky wrote three pieces with children's dolls in mind in his *Children's Album.* The first one, *The Sick Doll,* is definitely sad! The next piece is titled *The Dolls' Funeral,* and the last piece is *The New Doll.*

■ Emotion is an important aspect of the music.
■ *Rubato* is used.

Characteristics of the Romantic Era

We can sense the sad emotion in this piece by listening to the incessant repetition of the rhythm. Throughout the piece, the melody is interrupted with rests, as if someone were crying. Tchaikovsky added *tenuto* markings over the notes when he wanted the performer to be sure to play expressively by emphasizing them.

Measures 1-4:

Applying *rubato:*

This piece will be lovely, if played with rubato. Listen to the CD recording and hear how the tempo slows and then returns to the previous tempo with great fluidity. Practice the entire piece with the metronome, without any tempo fluctuations, and then turn off the metronome and sing along with the sad melody. With the added tenuto markings, you will be able to sense where the rubato can be. (You can turn to page 43 for additional practice strategies for creating a beautiful rubato.)

Practice Strategy

Adding pedal for an artistic effect:

Notice in the musical example above a way to pedal this piece that is different from the full score. Using the pedal this way, the melodic notes become slightly more sustained, creating a lingering and gloomy effect. Look at the pedaling that is marked in your full score, and decide with your teacher which sound you like better. Experiment with pressing the pedal halfway or a quarter of the way down to change the color of a phrase.

Practice Strategy

In the last eight measures, bring out the important moving melody in the left hand. Notice that the tenor and alto voices are the only two moving lines, so bringing these out over the other voices will add to the emotion of the piece.

Last eight measures:

THE SICK DOLL

Pyotr Ilyich Tchaikovsky
Op. 39, No. 7

Moderato, with expression (♩ = M.M. 100-104)

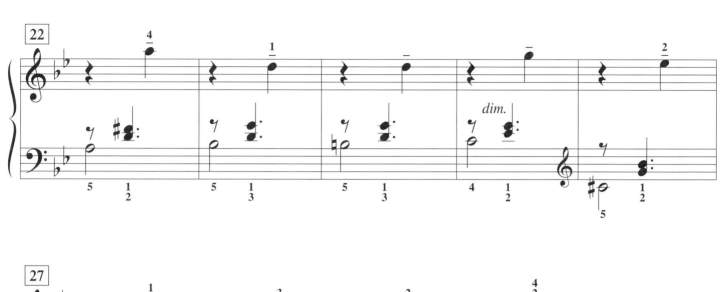

THE NEW DOLL

This is the third and happiest piece about dolls in Tchaikovsky's *Children's Album.* In the year this piece was composed, electricity in homes was becoming more common.

Characteristics of the Romantic Era

Characteristics of the era exemplified in this piece:

- Phrases of varying lengths.
- *The New Doll* is programmatic, which means that the energetic melody and rhythm of the piece create an image related to the title.

Practice Strategy

Shaping phrases:

This lively piece is made up of both long and short phrases. The dynamic markings in the long phrases show you where the phrase goals are. (A phrase goal is the place towards which the music naturally moves. In other words, the high point of the phrase is the phrase goal.)

Take a look at measures 17 to 25, listening to the CD. Notice that even though the short phrases are separated by rests, they form one long phrase which leads to the *forte* in measure 25. This is the high point of the entire piece. After this phrase goal is reached, the dynamics taper.

Sometimes singing the melody can help guide you in knowing how to shape each phrase, and understand how each phrase leads to the next phrase.

How to play repeated notes quickly and lightly:

Practice Strategy

The left hand must be played quickly, quietly, evenly, and lightly. In order to achieve this technique, drop into the keys with a loose wrist on the first beat. On the next beat, pull up from the keys with your wrist until you are playing on your fingertips. The second beat should sound lighter than the first one. Practice your left hand separately until the gesture is secure and comfortable, and you will not get tired!

THE NEW DOLL

Pyotr Ilyich Tchaikovsky
Op. 39, No. 6

N.B. All L.H. eighth notes should be played *staccato*.
In measure 17, *p* is found in the Tchaikovsky's autograph copy, but changed in the first edition by an editor to *mf*. You can decide which you prefer!

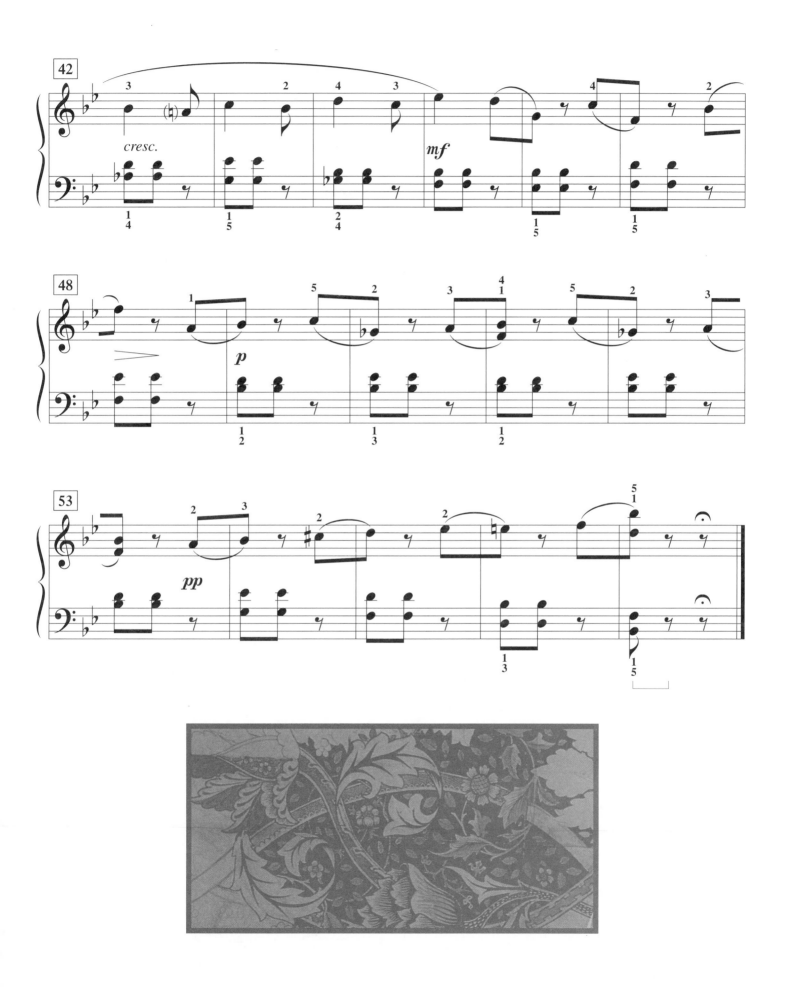

RUSSIAN SONG

**Tchaikovsky's music is strongly nationalistic, which means
that it evokes the strong character and sentiment of his native country.
When this piece was written in 1878, the United States White House
had its very first telephone installed.**

**Characteristics
of the
Romantic Era**

**Practice
Strategy**

A strong sense of rhythm helps to define this piece. Listen to the CD recording, and notice the steady beat and regular accents as well as the three–measure phrase structure. Notice the $\frac{2}{4}$ time signature and tap the rhythm of the piece. Is there any flexibility in the rhythm when you listen to it?

Chain-linking:

This practice strategy helps to increase accuracy and solidity.

Remember that in this practice strategy, you should always play slowly and deeply, pushing the keys to the bottom of the key bed.

Here's how it will work for you.

Play beats one and two:

*Make sure you stop
on the second beat!*

Repeat this until it is easy.
This practice strategy is to be used at a slow, "thoughtful" tempo.
Make sure that you do not play a chord until you know that you will play every note of it correctly.

Add another "link" onto the chain, playing from the first beat to the downbeat of measure two:

As you continue to add one or two beats to the chain, the phrase will become longer, and you will be confident that you are always playing the correct notes.

Use the "chain-linking" strategy for up to *three measures* of music, or one phrase, and then play the measures as one continuous musical phrase, feeling its forward motion.

Measures 1-3:

This practice strategy takes a lot of focus, but once you learn the chords, you will be able to play faster, with greater accuracy and more confidence!

Three fieldhands

Russian Song

Pyotr Ilyich Tchaikovsky
Op. 39, No. 12

N.B. The dynamics in measures 4, 6, and 8 are editorial.

OLD FRENCH SONG

Tchaikovsky traveled a great deal during his lifetime, so this piece is probably reminiscent of his time in Paris, France, where he went to hear some of his own music performed. The year this piece was written, the first American bicycle race was held in Boston, Massachusetts.

Characteristics of the Romantic Era

Characteristics of the era that reflect the traditions from the past exemplified in this piece:

- Use of traditional forms. For example, this piece has three sections, which makes it an ABA form. Mark this form (with a pencil!) in your score.
- Emotion and tenderness are important aspects of this piece.

It is interesting that for a piece that was a reminder of an earlier time, the composer chose to use more traditional forms and harmonies to reflect the past.

Practice Strategy

Balancing melody with accompaniment:

In the A section of this lovely piece, the melody is in the right hand while the left hand plays a *countermelody*, a new melody that accompanies the main melody.

Molto moderato, with feeling (♩ = M.M. 76-84)

In order to balance the main melody *over* the other parts, practice in the following ways:

1) Practice the right hand separately, listening to the rise and fall of the melody. Can you hum the melody *away* from the piano? If you can, then you really know the melody.

2) Practice the left hand separately, listening to the countermelody and accompaniment in the A section, and then the accompaniment in the B section. Be sure to shape the phrases!

3) Play the left hand much louder than the right hand, feeling more weight from your arm and hand going to the bottom of the keys. Ask yourself, "Did I make enough of a contrast between the A and B sections with respect to the articulations?"

4) Next, play the right hand more loudly than the left hand, again feeling more weight from your arm and hand going to the bottom of the keys. Listen again for the shaping of each phrase.

Does the piece sound better if the right hand or the left hand is louder? If you are playing it correctly, balancing the right hand over the left hand is the sound and approach you will want to take for the entire piece. However, be sure to listen for a contrast in articulations and an interesting countermelody in the left hand.

Playing outside during the Romantic era. 1858

Old French Song

Pyotr Ilyich Tchaikovsky
Op. 39, No. 16

Molto moderato, with feeling ($\quad$ = M.M. 76-84)

N.B. The slurs from measures 2-3, 4-5, 8-9, 10-11, and 12-13 are editorial.

WALTZ

The waltz developed from the "German Dances," pieces that were written
by composers from Austria during the Classical era. The waltz became
widely popular throughout Europe in the late eighteenth century
and became even more popular in the nineteenth century.

**Characteristics
of the
Romantic Era**

Observe in this piece the use of *rubato*.

Listen to the recording to observe how *rubato* can be applied while maintaining the sense
of pulse.

**Practice
Strategy**

Practicing a waltz bass:

In order to play the leaps in the left hand correctly and evenly, use the following strategy:

Play every downbeat, and then move your hand and silently *prepare* your fingers over the
notes of the next beat (circled below). Only when you know that your fingers are on the
correct keys should you actually *play* the notes. Use this strategy for every measure. In
time, playing a waltz bass will be very easy for you.

Measures 1-5:

In order to feel one beat per bar, drop into the downbeat with your left hand and then
immediately lift off and move to the second beat. On the second and third beats, play
lightly and on your fingertips!

Measures 1-5:

Drop on the downbeat and lift immediately.

Practicing with the metronome:

Practice
Strategy

- Practice short segments of the piece at the following metronome speeds. You might wish to use a different tempo each day for fun as you practice.

♩ = 88   ♩. = 58   ♩. = 69

- Using the metronome helps to develop an inner sense of pulse and is one of the best ways to increase the tempo gradually without losing control.

- Practice hands separately first, then hands together. It's a good idea to stop occasionally on different beats in the measure to make sure you are lining up your playing with the tick of the metronome.

- Once you have practiced with the metronome and know that you can play the waltz evenly and steadily, you can turn off the metronome and play with more freedom and rubato. Listen to the recording and write in your score where this sense of freedom takes place.

Reindeer racing in Russia

WALTZ

Pyotr Ilyich Tchaikovsky
Op. 39, No. 9

78

FF1440

MARCH OF THE WOODEN SOLDIERS

Characteristics of the Romantic Era

In this piece, the harmonic language is expanded for added color. Tchaikovsky uses not only tonic, subdominant and dominant chords, but also more colorful harmonies that are not part of the key, as shown below:

Measures 20-24:

Practice Strategy

Playing dotted rhythms:

The following sixteenth-note rhythmic pattern is found throughout this piece.

Moderato (♩ = M.M. 112-126)

With the metronome set at ♪=100, count out loud while tapping the following rhythms. Continue to count and tap each line without stopping so that you feel the forward direction of the rhythm.

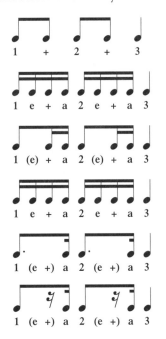

Continue each line without stopping!

The rhythm of ♫ is the same as ♪𝄾♪ except that the first is held for a longer length of time, since it is slurred and does not have a rest.

After you can do this easily, increase the metronome tempo to ♪ = 120, and then ♩ = 100, and ♩ = 120. Isolate and practice the measures in your score that have sixteenth-note patterns. Playing each measure correctly four times in a row will help you to play this piece with ease and confidence!

Getting ready for a performance:

Practice Strategy

When you feel that you are almost ready for a performance, here is what you can do to ensure complete confidence. During one of your practice sessions, play your piece once through without stopping, exactly how you would like to play it in public with respect to tempo and sound. After you have played the piece, mark with a star any measure that wasn't completely to your liking, like this:

Measures 17-28:

The marked measures then, will be the only measures that you will practice during one of your practice sessions. Practice a particular measure in five ways, and then check off the corresponding box:

☐ 1) Hands separately. If you spend time practicing, listening, and focusing on one hand at a time, it will really help your confidence. You will know that you understand the piece.
☐ 2) Slowly with the metronome, hands together.
☐ 3) Three times slowly followed by one time up to tempo.
☐ 4) One measure plus the next downbeat; eight times in a row, correctly.
☐ 5) Starting one measure before the measure you marked and playing to the next downbeat.

The next day, erase the stars you marked in the day before and try the practice strategy again. Over a few days you will identify and work on all of the areas which need special attention.

March of the Wooden Soldiers

Pyotr Ilyich Tchaikovsky
Op. 39, No. 5

(a) The downbeats of measures 6 and 14 may be played with the R.H.

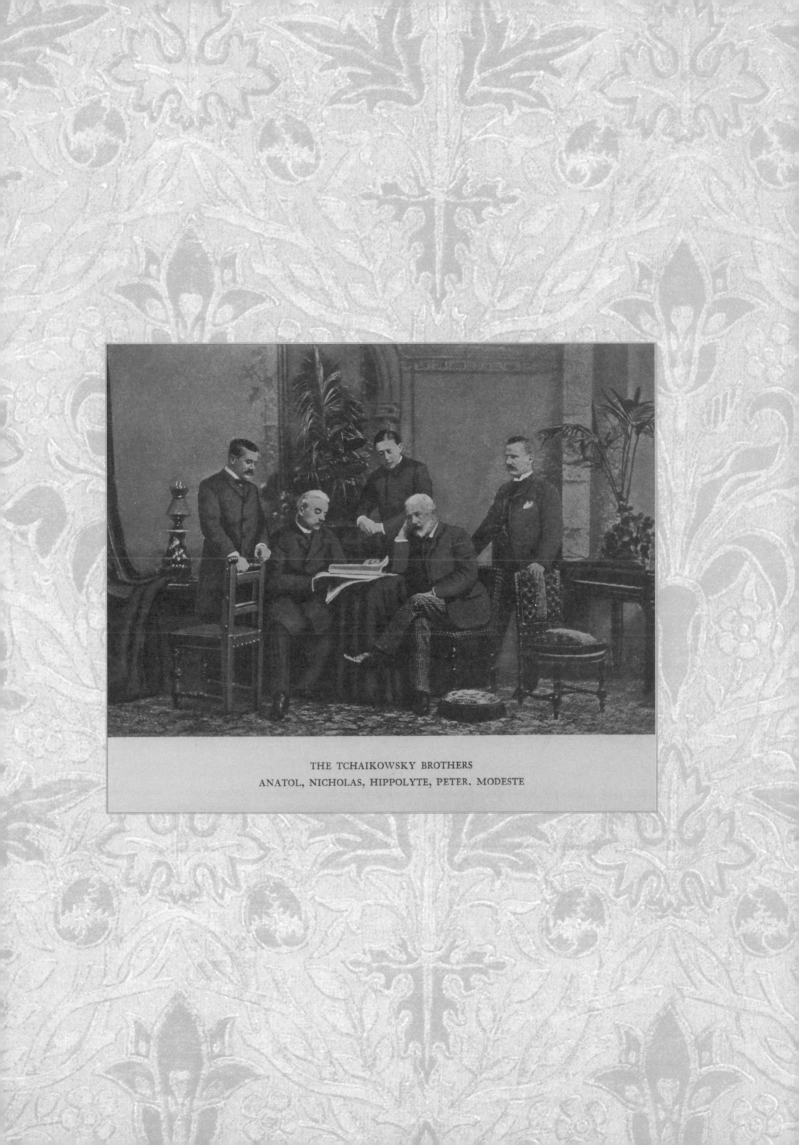

THE TCHAIKOWSKY BROTHERS
ANATOL, NICHOLAS, HIPPOLYTE, PETER. MODESTE

Volume One – Repertoire with their Sources

Sources consulted for this edition:

Schubert, Franz. <u>Werke. Kritische durchgesehen Gesammtausgabe</u>. Leipzig: Breitkopf & Härtel, 1884-1897.

Schumann, Robert. <u>Werke</u>. Edited by Clara Schumann. Leipzig: Breitkopf & Härtel, 1881-1893. Reprinted by Gregg Press, Farnborough, England, 1967-68.

Schumann, Robert. <u>Album for the Young</u>. Edited by Gary Busch. Fort Lauderdale: The FJH Music Company, 2004. (Much of the background information for each piece from Schumann's Album for the Young is taken from this Urtext edition by Dr. Gary Busch.)

Tchaikovsky, Pyotr. <u>Children's Album, Op. 39</u>. Edited by Thomas Kohlhase. Fingering and notes on interpretation by Alexandr Satz. Wiener Urtext Edition. Vienna: Musikverlag Ges. m.b. H. & Co., K.G, 2000.

Tchaikovsky, Pyotr. <u>Complete Works, volume IV</u>. Edited by Victor Sumarokov and Sergei Chebotaryov. Budapest: Könemann Music, 1998.

GLOSSARY OF MUSICAL TERMS
Tempo markings

Allegro	*Allegretto*	*Moderato*	*Andante*	*Grave*
cheerful, bright, faster than *allegretto*	same feeling as *allegro*, but not as fast	a moderate tempo	walking tempo	slow, solemn

Accompaniment – a musical background for a principal part. In the Romantic era, the accompaniment can be in another hand, or played with the melody in the same hand. The accompaniment provides harmony for the melody.

allegro assai – a tempo marking that means "even faster than *allegro*." In Italian, *assai* means "a lot of," or "plenty."

a tempo – return to the regular tempo, especially after a *ritardando*.

Binary form – a piece built in two parts (AB); the first part sometimes ends on the tonic but most of the time ends on the dominant chord (V), and the second part ends on the tonic. Both parts are usually marked to be repeated before going on.

cantabile – an Italian term for "singing."

Countermelody – a musical line different from that of the primary melody. A countermelody can be part of an accompaniment.

Chorale – originally meant a hymn of the German protestant church. In piano music, composers used the term as a title to create the mood of the atmosphere in a church.

Chordal – a piece in which three or more tones are played simultaneously.

Diatonic scale – based on an octave divided into five whole steps and two half steps. The major and natural minor scales are diatonic. In a major scale, the two half steps are between the 3rd and 4th as well as the 7th and 8th degrees of the scale, without any chromatic alterations. For example, a diatonic A-major scale has the following notes: A B C♯ D E F♯ G♯ A.

Downbeat – the first beat of a full measure, or the downward motion of a conductor's hand.

Ecossaise – a quick country dance in $\frac{2}{4}$ time.

espressivo – an Italian term that means to play with "meaning and emotion."

Grace note – a small, ornamental note or set of notes played before a principal note, usually before the beat.

grazioso – An Italian term for "graceful."

Homophonic texture – a melody supported by harmonies. The melodic voice is often in the right hand with chords in the left, to create the harmony. It can also be done the other way around, melody in the left hand and chords above.

legato – smooth and connected, without any interruption between the notes.

Ländler – a slow dance from Austria, usually in $\frac{3}{4}$ time.

maestoso – an Italian term for "majestic."

March – a piece with simple and strong rhythm, and regular phrasing. The Italian term *alla marcia* means "in the style of a march."

meno mosso – an Italian term meaning "less motion" or "less quickly."

Monophonic texture – a bare melodic line, in single notes or octaves.

(N.B.) Nota Bene – a Latin phrase meaning, "mark well." Used to point out something important.

Phrase goal – the place toward which the music naturally moves, just as, when we speak, our sentences move toward a word with slightly more emphasis or volume than others. Let your ear be your guide and follow this rise of melody toward a goal. After arrival at its goal, the phrase naturally tapers.

Polyphonic texture – music with several lines (two or more) instead of a single melody and an accompaniment.

rubato – the Italian word for "stolen," indicating to stretch or broaden the tempo. The time taken is made up within the same phrase or shortly thereafter.

sforzando – an Italian term (abbreviated *sf*)which means to create a forced accent on a note or chord.

tenuto – a note that should be emphasized by holding and sustaining it to its full value.

Ternary form – music that has three sections, ABA or ABC.

Upbeat (anacrusis) – one or more notes in an incomplete measure occurring before the first bar line of a piece or section of music; sometimes called a *pickup*.

Waltz – a dance in triple time, slow or fast, with one beat in the bar. It first appeared in the late eighteenth century as a development from the German Dances. The waltz was developed primarily by Viennese composers. Precursors to the waltz were the Baroque *allemande* and *minuet*.